Windjammers
Lighthouses
and Other Treasures
of the Maine Coast

Windjammers anchoring in company is more the rule than the exception . . . Merchantile *and* Heritage

Windjammers Lighthouses

and Other Treasures

of the Maine Coast

photography by
Frank M. Chillemi

for Roberta & Elliot

Frank M Chill

Down East Books

Copyright © 2005 by Frank M. Chillemi

Designed by Harrah Lord, Yellow House Studio, Rockport, Maine

Printed in China by Oceanic Graphic Printing, Inc.

5   4   3   2   1

Down East Books

Camden, Maine

A division of Down East Enterprise,

publisher of *Down East* magazine.

Book orders: 800-685-7962

www.downeastbooks.com

ISBN: 0-89272-680-6

Library of Congress Control Number: 2004117842

DEDICATION

Novelist James Baldwin once commented that
"Everyone wants an artist on the wall or on
the mantelpiece, but nobody wants one
in the house." This book is dedicated
to my wife Rose—who fully
understands the meaning
of Mr. Baldwin's words,
but keeps letting me
in the house
anyway.

ACKNOWLEDGEMENTS

The journey to any accomplishment can be made a little less arduous by seeking out, studying with, and learning from those masters whose work you truly admire. For me, that meant following a path to photographers Joyce Tenneson, Bill Eppridge, and Benjamin Mendlowitz.

The sheer amount of work that goes into the care of any structure that lives on, or near, the sea is really something that must be experienced to be understood. It's a devilish combination of rusted bolts, busted knuckles, colorful language, heartache, heartburn, commercial paints, and industrial-strength stomach medicine. This book would never have been possible were it not for the people who work tirelessly to keep the pieces of history portrayed within these pages there for all of us: Capt's. Jon Finger and Anne Mahle (schooner *J. & E. Riggin*), Capt. Bill Brown (pinky schooner *Summertime*), Capt. Sean O'Connor (schooner *Lazy Jack*), Capt's. Ken, Ellen, and Noah Barnes (schooner *Stephen Taber*), Mr. Ben Russell (Hendricks Head Light), Capt. Garth Wells (schooner *Lewis R. French*), Capt. Brenda Walker (schooner *Isaac H. Evans*), Mr. & Mrs. George E. Gans III (Pumpkin Island Light), Capt. Ray, and Ann Williamson (schooners *Grace Bailey*, *Merchantile*, and *Mistress*), Capt. Barry King, (schooner *Mary Day*), The American Lighthouse Foundation (Pemaquid Point and Rockland Breakwater Lights), Capt. Neal Parker (schooner *Wendameen*), Capt. Owen, and Cathie Dorr (schooner *Nathaniel Bowditch*), Capt's. Doug and Linda Lee (schooner *Heritage*), St. George Historical Society (Marshall Point Light), Capt. Steve Pagels (schooner *Margaret Todd* and bugeye ketch *Little Jennie*), Tabor Academy Headmaster Jay Stroud (schooner *Tabor Boy*), Capt's. R. Files and P. Degaeta (schooner *Victory Chimes*), Capt. Robert, and Dawn Tassi (schooner *Timberwind*), Capt. John Foss (schooner *American Eagle*), Capt. Paul, and Kris Williamson (schooner *Ellida*), the town of Castine, Maine (Dice Head Light), Capt. Gordon, and Kathryn Baxter (schooner *Kathryn B.*) and Capt. Mike McHenry (windjammer *Angelique*). In addition, I'd like to express my appreciation to Capt. Havilah Hawkins, Capt. David Allen, and to the United States Coast Guard.

INTRODUCTION

There is a special connection between mankind and the sea; a connection that lies deep within us. Scientists, historians, and theologians offer many varied explanations for this, and all of them are correct to a greater or lesser degree. Imagine for a moment a place where the sea meets a complex, rugged, and stunningly beautiful shoreline. Combine all this with some of the most magical light on earth. As a final touch, add some of mankind's most enduring and historic creations in the form of majestic windjammers and towering lighthouses. What you now have is a good idea of what you'll find along the more than twenty-five hundred total miles of bays, islands, and narrow glacier-etched peninsulas that make up the coast of Maine.

It's been my privilege to work, study, and teach in this area since 1988. There is an overwhelming sense of place that fulfills a deep yearning in me when I'm here. That same feeling tugs at my heart while I'm away. In my time along these shores, there have been many opportunities to make photographs that help me express my strong spiritual feelings for this coast that, year after year, feels more like home.

Some of my experiences, however, are best conveyed within these few paragraphs. The one that had perhaps the greatest effect on me was the quiet emotion of a workshop participant one cool October morning at Pemaquid Point Light. My group arrived early and set up our tripods and other equipment by flashlight. As we stood in the pre-dawn glow, I couldn't help noticing that one lady had begun to cry softly. Thinking she may be experiencing some easily correctable camera problem, I walked over quietly and offered her help. What this woman shared with me came as a revelation. She was about to witness her very first sunrise! The gravity of her statement took a long moment to completely sink in. It was impossible for me to imagine how that could ever be for a full-grown adult. A poet might have found a way to respond to her with words. This photographer could not. I gently touched her hand then slowly backed away to allow her some privacy as the colors of the morning began painting themselves across the ever-brightening sky. Later on we spoke again. She confessed to being a bit embarrassed. Now the words came to me in a steady flow. It was easy to assure her that what she had experienced was an intellectual, emotional, and creative breakthrough. My student still had the rest of her life to "catch up"…and she should celebrate that! She promised me that witnessing this sunrise had been her first, with many more to follow.

Another participant had to overcome severe physical problems to sail with us on a photo cruise. She had always wanted to come and make pictures along the Maine coast, but her disability had prevented her from doing that alone. The idea of spending a week doing what she had dreamed of in the company of like-minded individuals provided the inspiration and the opportunity she needed. The effort this woman had to make every day just to be with us was amazing. It was inspiring to see the rest of the group extending themselves, in small yet important ways, to ease her burden throughout the trip. Heightened sensitivity is a wonderful thing.

OVERVIEW

This is primarily a book of photographs. My plan from the beginning was not to load it down with a lot of heavy technical material. I would like to share some general concepts that have worked effectively for me over the years and that may be helpful to you as well.

The subject of camera gear is always of great concern when people plan any trip where photography will be important to them. Equipment buffs can be quickly disappointed because nautical landscape work actually favors a simple approach. Any camera that will do what you ask it to, without getting in your way, will work just fine. Add to that a sturdy tripod, perhaps a few filters, lots of film or memory capacity, and you're pretty much ready to go. That's not to say your exotic equipment won't be useful . . . it's just a reminder that you should not pass up a trip to the coast of Maine because your camera bag can be lifted with one hand. In fact, being a photographer is not even required. One young lady came on a photo cruise just to be with her father. "He's the photographer, I'm just here to relax and enjoy the food." She began the trip that way, but throughout the week her opinion changed as her interest grew. By our third day she had borrowed a camera and joined the group. Both dad and his daughter went home with some very expressive pictures.

Photographic technique is the next topic. Volumes have been written about composition, framing, subject placement, and such. My approach for this type of photography is a time-honored principle: Try to be at the right place . . . at the right light. Behind this, of course, lies a complex series of thought and emotional processes. I encourage my students to get a feel for the place and then let that 'feel' guide them. It really does work. Expressive photography is all about conveying how we see and react to the world around us.

Beyond technique lies the true heart and spirit of your photographs. The ships, and especially the lighthouses, in this book are very spiritual creations. They can have a profound effect on you. The most direct way to make that connection is simply to spend some time learning about your subjects before you ever reach for your camera. Knowing the history and some of the tall tales and salty stories surrounding a vessel is more important than remembering her length, sail plan, and gross displacement. The same is true with lighthouses. They are very special places. Lives have been saved—and lives have been lost—at these places. Learning a few of their stories, legends, and myths will help you develop and understand your feelings as you go about your work.

As a last item before dividing this discussion into two distinct activities, please allow me a moment to mention your silent collaborator. I'm certain that the quality of this land, this water, and this light quite simply could not have just happened. John Denver beautifully spoke of a higher being as "our mother the earth." It is She who provides or withholds the exquisite light, the clouds, the waves, and the fog. He described the wind as Her whisper. Giving this higher being a gesture of recognition and appreciation for Her help has become very important to me. In my opinion, four lines from one of John's songs, say it best.

Welcome the wind and the wisdom she offers,
Follow her summons when she calls again,
In your heart and your spirit let the breezes surround you,
Lift up your voice then and sing with the wind.

Those lines, spoken softly while preparing to make photographs, provide me with a small way of showing that appreciation. For what it's worth, I'm convinced She listens.

PHOTOGRAPHS MADE FROM THE LAND

In today's unsure times, it's just natural to seek the reassurance of things we see as secure and dependable. Perhaps that explains why one of the most timeless and enduring icons of such stability throughout history has been the lighthouse. From the very first one, built outside Alexandria, Egypt, around 280 B.C., these long-standing, rock-steady sentinels have always been emblematic of safety, security, and, often times, home. Peter Ralston of Maine's Island Institute aptly described them as "ageless, powerful, potent places." They are, both literally and emotionally, a light ahead in the darkness. America's shorelines and inland waterways are populated with unique examples of these historic structures. The coast of Maine, with its many offshore islands laden with dangerous shoals and submerged ledges, has more than sixty of these majestic beacons.

There seems to be an overly constricted set of rules that photographers sometimes feel obligated to follow when working with lighthouses. Perhaps it's because they have been photographed so often by so many people. That in itself should not get in your way. Try to remember three things as you are walking towards one of these lights: the conditions you experience today are unique, they will be different tomorrow, and most importantly, this lighthouse has never been seen through your eyes before! Trying to copy what you've seen in magazines and on postcards is the easy way of doing things. A far better way is just to let each experience have its effect on you. Then make your photographs based on those effects. My way of working may again seem overly simple: approach with respect, work quietly without attracting attention, share the experience with students, and leave with a few additional pieces of garbage besides my own.

Scheduling a photography trip in Maine does require some care, however. The tidal range can run more than twenty feet. This can affect your pictures drastically. Vast expanses of mud flats are exposed and then hidden by the water in a very short span of time. The light along the coast is excellent most of the time. It's often breathtaking in the early morning and late afternoon. Planning your visit so that high tide coincides with these times is a good way to get your trip off to a great start. Combining that with the time of the full moon adds two additional advantages. The first is that the tides are just a little higher. The second is that the moon itself can add an exciting addition to your photos. My personal preference is to work in the early morning. There is far less going on along the coast, and usually less going on in the image you are composing. That lone lobster boat moving through your frame is always going to be more expressive than the same composition filled with personal watercraft buzzing about in the afternoon.

Making pictures from the land gives a photographer great flexibility. There are so many different locations to choose from that you should never run out of things to photograph. You will feel an immediate emotional connection with certain areas that you simply will not with others. As creative people, we understand that this situation is completely natural. Coming across another vista only a few minutes farther on is a powerful reason to want to photograph along these shores.

I chose the featured lighthouse for this book strictly for its emotional effect on me. Hendricks Head Light is not the biggest, nor the brightest, and certainly not the most famous light along the Maine coast. Its connection to this photographer can be felt much more easily than it can ever be explained. Hendricks Head is the only fully operational light in the U.S. Coast Guard system that is privately owned and maintained. Ben Russell is its owner and he was very generous in allowing me to work there.

PHOTOGRAPHS MADE FROM THE WATER

In the patches of thick fog you could hear her coming. The mist can play tricks on your ability to judge direction, but we knew a ship was close. I told my students to be ready. As she broke into view off our starboard bow, there was no mistaking her elegant line and majestic image—the schooner *Heritage*. She is but one of the many windjammers that call this coast home. Many more visit these waters frequently. A number of these vessels have deep historical significance. The schooners *Lewis R. French* and *Stephen Taber* are both more than one hundred thirty-four years old. Some, like the schooner *Isaac H. Evans,* have been designated National Historic Landmarks. Their histories are as varied and different as their hull shapes and sail plans. Twenty-four of these ships are portrayed within these pages.

Photographing from the water is always a challenge. The constantly changing conditions will keep you on your toes. The speed at which some of these sleek windjammers can approach is very surprising. The advantage of actually being out there is that you can experience for yourself the grace of these ships under full sail. My two favorite ways of working are from a windjammer itself, and from a kayak.

Let's look at the windjammers first. Along the Maine coast there are numerous vessels conducting trips with durations from as little as two hours to as long as a week or more. A schooner trip is one of the best vacations you and your family will ever enjoy. The sailing is fun, the other passengers are friendly, the food is excellent, and the opportunities to make exciting photographs are pretty much limitless. Before breakfast there is always time to get out in a sturdy rowboat to photograph your ship or other windjammers nearby. Anchoring in company with other vessels is a common practice among schooner captains along the coast. Once underway there are all kinds of things happening. Sailing side by side with another windjammer is always more the rule than the exception. Passing offshore of historic lighthouses and other points of interest is a regular occurrence. You will find your captain and crew as enthusiastic about your pictures as you are. Let the captain know in advance that making photographs is an important part of your vacation. Most will be eager to discuss the day's anticipated course with you, and what you might be able to expect. Keep in mind that your ship will really "go where the wind takes her," and that an anticipated course is just that. Most of these windjammers are built of heavy wood. They were constructed for strength and durability. That makes them some of the most stable platforms for a passenger to enjoy or a photographer to work from.

DENISE LOVE-ADAMS PHOTO

Kayaks are my favorite way to get out on the water. Sleek, silent, and close to the surface, they can go where other boats simply cannot. In a kayak you are not on the water as much as you are a part of it. You get a stronger feel for the conditions, the currents, and the wind. This raises your senses and makes understanding your subject and your composition easier. In addition, a kayak draws very little attention to itself. One of the most disappointing things that can happen is to get a beautiful wind-jammer about to pass you in gorgeous light only to have all the passengers hanging on the rail, waving at you. Most of the time that little boat, resting just outside the marked channel, will go unnoticed.

The featured windjammer for this edition is the Schooner *J. & E. Riggin.* Selecting just one vessel for its emotional value alone would have been beyond my ability. My choice was made from a much more practical vantage point. Capt.'s Jon Finger and Anne Mahle host our annual autumn photography cruise. My opportunities to portray this long, low, fast—and very very black—schooner have simply been the most plentiful.

We find ourselves in a world today made up of ever-increasing uncertainty. It is also a world made up of increasing self-importance. At the same time this is a world that, strangely enough, seems more and more . . . to be made up less and less . . . of any real adventure. Making the photographs for this book has provided me with a distinct departure from much of that. There have been many opportunities to experience the unique sense of place that makes the Maine coast so special. I've tasted its immense natural beauty as well as the cooperation from all the people involved with these pictures. I've been blessed at times with the gift of real generosity from total strangers. There have been many adventures along the way. A few of them have been greater than I ever would have imagined. It's my pleasure to share at least a small part of this with all of you.

Windjammers . . .

Long, low, and very very black, the schooner J. & E. Riggin moves through the water with an unmistakable grace.

J. & E. Riggin's *captains,*
Jon Finger and Anne Mahle.

Pumpkin Island Light was built not to welcome sailors, but to warn them of the dangerous ledges submerged just off shore.

The Riggin's first mate, Dan Engel. The future of these windjammers is with young career sailors like Dan. That future is in good hands.

With her foremast arching from the force of the wind, she pushed through the water, spray flying everywhere . . . the bugeye ketch Little Jennie.

Summertime *is one of very few of this type of design, known as the pinky schooner.* 25

Summertime's *captain, Bill Brown.*

The schooner Lazy Jack runs short day sails from Maine harbors such as Camden and Boothbay. These trips offer a great chance for people to experience a windjammer firsthand.

30 *Crashing through big swells just southwest of Owls Head Harbor . . . schooner* Stephen Taber.

*Two legends along the Maine Coast are Stephen Taber's captains,
Ken and Ellen Barnes. Built in 1871, the Taber is now in the capable hands of their son Noah.*

The schooner Grace Bailey is one of a trio of windjammers based in Camden. 31

She had no idea of my presence and yet she sailed right under my vantage point in
beautiful morning light . . . Mistress.

The annual Great Schooner Race is one of the highlights of the windjammer season along the Maine coast . . . Wendameen *and* Merchantile.

On our way to Boothbay Harbor from Rockland, she swept past us.
The American Eagle is one of the most elegant schooners on any coast.

The late Capt. Havilah Hawkins, Mary Day's designer and first captain. Besides being an excellent sailor, Capt. Hawkins was an inventor, painter, sculptor, entrepreneur, philosopher, a great friend, and a master storyteller.

Designed and built expressly for carrying passengers, the Mary Day looks fast even when standing still.

The three-masted schooner Victory Chimes *has been described as big and bulky, but that must have been by someone who has never seen her in the morning's first light.*

*Victory Chimes . . . unmistakable,
even by just the tops of her masts.*

*On her way back to her home port of Rockland, Victory Chimes
passes off the Rockland Breakwater Light.*

41

42　　　*With her unique Marconi-rigged mainsail set close to the wind, the* Ellida *quickly overtook us.*

Named for the father of modern navigation, the Nathaniel Bowditch
is sleek, graceful, and wicked fast. 43

44   Heritage *passed just off Rockland Breakwater Light, coming home on her last trip of the season.*

46   *She is the sail-training schooner of the Tabor Academy of Marion, Massachusetts . . . Tabor Boy.*

Tabor Boy *at anchor in Sherman Cove, just outside Camden Harbor.* 47

48   *A short time after sunset, the schooner* Timberwind *lay at anchor, quiet and serene.*

*Attracted to her mainsails left in their hoisted position, we found Timberwind
tucked safely into Sherman Cove, near Camden Harbor.*   49

Classic in design, yet relatively newly constructed, the Margaret Todd *is the first four-masted schooner to work the Maine coast in more than fifty years.*

Another of the day-sailors offering short trips of varying length, the yacht Shantih II.   51

52   Isaac H. Evans *is passed by* American Eagle *off Ram Island, near Boothbay Harbor.*

Pre-dawn light in Tenants Harbor washes over the schooner Isaac H. Evans.　　53

Launched into Christmas Cove in 1871, the schooner Lewis R. French *has worked continuously, at many trades. She continues that tradition to this day.*

Bearing down upon us at about as fast as she can go, this pass by the Lewis R. French
served up more adventure than this photographer would ever have bargained for. 55

Late afternoon aboard the Lewis R. French.

Three windjammers sailing in company on Penobscot Bay,
. . . Angelique, Heritage, and Isaac H. Evans.   57

On a bold, clear morning in a freshening breeze, the three-masted schooner Kathryn B. *came up behind us, with the* Nathaniel Bowditch *in the distance.*

On a perfectly calm summer morning, three windjammers lay at anchor in Wooden Boat Cove ...

60   Angelique, Heritage, *and* Grace Bailey.

Though much more European in design than other ships along the Maine coast,
Angelique is just as beautiful.   61

Rafted together in the morning fog . . . American Eagle, Nathaniel Bowditch, Summertime, *and* Mistress.

A common sight one hundred years ago, but very rare today:
Twenty-nine tall ships at anchor in their natural habitat.   63

Lighthouses . . .

Not the biggest, brightest, or the most famous light along the Maine coast, she is, for me at least,
the most compelling . . . Hendricks Head.

Sunset at Hendricks Head Light.

Pemaquid Point Light is perhaps the most photographed lighthouse on the east coast, certainly one of the most unique and beautiful.   69

72   *Bass Harbor Head Light is a fairly good distance from any beaten path, but it's worth the trip.*

*From his office in New York City in 1789, President George Washington ordered
construction of the very first lighthouse in Maine: Portland Head.* 73

Visible for miles due to her height above the water, Owls Head Light guides sailors to both the harbor that bears her name and to Rockland Harbor as well.

Just outside the town of York sits Cape Neddick Light.
She is one of the most popular tourist spots in Maine.

Cape Neddick Light in her holiday decorations, an annual tradition.   77

Not far from the working harbor at Port Clyde, Marshall Point Light
is one of those places where you can feel the history all around you.

Nestled just outside of Camden Harbor, Curtis Island has become a favorite nesting place for bald eagles.

Built high on a hill above the waters near Castine, Dice Head Light rises boldly,
nestled among the evergreens.

Other Treasures . . .

Once a down-n-dirty working harbor, Camden is now a tourist town with something for everyone.
It is home to some of the finest ships and tastiest clam chowder anywhere on the Maine coast.

A lone oarsman makes his way across Outer Camden Harbor. 89

90   *The sun begins peeking over the horizon at the mouth of Camden Harbor.*

*Countless hours of building, rebuilding, maintenance, and repair
go into keeping a windjammer seaworthy.*   91

92   *The view from Laite Beach is an ever-changing one.*

Weather along these shores comes and goes at its own will.
This is a clearing summer storm over Rockport Harbor.   93

94 *Our Lady Queen of Peace Church overlooks beautiful Boothbay Harbor.*

The schooners Lewis R. French *and* Stephen Taber *were both built in 1871. Here, they are shown rafted together during the Boothbay Harbor Windjammer Festival.*

*The quickly receding tide leaves a veritable buffet on a sandbar just off
Laite Beach, on Outer Camden Harbor.*